T0195008

THE KING'S BUNKER GAME

A Defense Strategy For Beginners

Robert W. Bradshaw

THE KING'S BUNKER GAME
A DEFENSE STRATEGY FOR BEGINNERS

iUniverse books may be ordered through booksellers or by contacting:

iUniverse
1663 Liberty Drive
Bloomington, IN 47403
www.iuniverse.com
844-349-9409

ISBN: 978-1-6632-3768-2 (sc)
ISBN: 978-1-6632-3790-3 (hc)
ISBN: 978-1-6632-3769-9 (e)

Library of Congress Control Number: 2022905871

Print information available on the last page.

iUniverse rev. date: 06/24/2022

To honor the memory of my mother, Joanne Hardeman Powers Bradshaw (1930–2021), who taught me the virtue of fortitude: Never quit—never, never, never.

PREFACE

Why I Play Chess

My wife and I raised our two children, and they graduated from high school and then went to college. After our youngest went away to college, there was a significant amount of time in the evenings that I could spend, so I thought about various productive projects because time is the most valuable item that humans possess.

A Masonic Lodge asked me to dinner, and I knew on my first visit that I wanted to be a Freemason because Freemasonry was the perfect benevolent project for me to spend my time. Self-improvement and making the world a better place was much more of a prudent choice than spending my evenings playing video games or watching sports.

When COVID-19 hit, my Masonic Lodge no longer met in person in the evenings, so I was once again forced to determine the most prudent way to spend my time. Chess was the answer. I joined Chess.com in the first week of October in 2020, and a few days later, the TV series *Queen's Gambit* aired. I took many lessons and played many games on Chess.com. Then, in January 2021, I joined the Chess Club & Scholastic Center of Atlanta.

On one of my Google searches for "chess," I discovered the MasterClass series, which provides education from legendary titans and all-time greats in specific industries and fields. Since I grew up with Garry Kasparov, I sought his chess instruction and coaching. As a birthday gift to myself, I took my first MasterClass lesson in chess from Garry Kasparov on February 21, 2021.

Why I Wrote This Book

From February until June 2021, I was taking chess lessons from a grand master coach on a weekly basis, and my grand master's assignment was to play many puzzles and at least two or three games per week so that he could evaluate my progress. His class was one hour per week, and the puzzles and games took about three hours per week for a total of four hours per week. However, the actual time displacement, when considering preparation and recovery time, was closer to seven or eight hours per week. Additionally, there was the challenge of transitioning into the chess space from my profession from which I derive my income to take care of my family.

My chess journey forever changed on Memorial Day when my mother went into the hospital where she stayed in the ICU until June 7. My mother died with me holding her hand at home on June 9. I continued to play chess and take lessons from my grand master with increasing difficulty because I did not have time to dedicate to chess while I attended to family matters.

On July 23, I informed my grand master that I would be taking a "sabbatical" from his coaching. The next day, July 24, was my mother's birthday, and she would have been ninety-one years old. As I listened to Brad Paisley in concert that day, it dawned on me that part of my mother's legacy was her virtue of fortitude (never quit), which was also an attribute of Winston Churchill. I knew that I needed to do three things. (1) I still wanted to play and contribute to chess, the greatest game in the world, past, present, and future. (2) I wanted to honor my mother's memory and legacy. (3) I had to figure out a way to manage the grieving process. My collective subconscious suggested that I could accomplish all of these feats by identifying a unique strategy, writing a book, and dedicating it to my mother.

I became almost completely obsessed with chess to the point that I was borderline psychotic. Ironically, this was needed as my therapy in the grieving process. From July 27 to August 17, I played five hundred games on Chess.com (yes, I have proof and handwritten notes of each game) to validate my thesis of the King's Bunker Strategy. At times during those three weeks, I felt that I was slipping into another reality or dimension, and I definitely understand why many avid chess players and advanced theoretical physicists go crazy. I needed this experience to let go of my mother and to purge my emotional pain of her death. As with the duality of life, I was burying my mother, putting her to rest in my heart, mind, and soul, and at the same time, I was raising my mother so that her legacy would continue to live. Thus, I consider my mother's legacy, the virtue of fortitude, as a gift to me, and I want to share that gift with the world by writing and publishing *The King's Bunker Game.*

Garry Kasparov: The Greatest Chess Player in History

Garry Kasparov is the greatest world chess champion of all time. For twenty-one years, from 1984 until 2005, Kasparov was ranked number one in the world, which is the longest number-one ranking in human history (Wikipedia).

> If you can appreciate that chess is an immensely rich game (10 to the 120th power in possible patterns), then you can keep finding new ideas to make you happy. Nothing could make you happier than to find new ways to solve puzzles and to make yourself more engaged in this endless process of exploration. While people talk about one person being more talented, but another being a hard worker, hard work is a talent because hard work means that you keep going and keep fighting. You know how *not* to quit under pressure even if you fail and don't succeed. You keep going and keep pushing. (MasterClass)

> Know who you are and play to your natural instincts. Are you type one: aggressive decisions, big, (bold) and dynamic style? (Are) you type two: cautious (decisions), vigilant, slower (and gain) small advantages while waiting for (your) opponent's mistakes? It is no secret that you have to practice the talent of hard work. You have to keep practicing until learning patterns becomes intuitive.

Playing chess will enable you to find new and creative answers and solutions in your everyday life (which will make you happy.) (MasterClass)

Garry Kasparov's Secret to Success

Kasparov believes the secret to success in chess is (1) hard work, which was taught by his mother and (2) never quit, which he learned from Winston Churchill. His memory was good but not photographic and he usually ate smoked salmon and steak and drank tonic water before a game of chess because protein provides three times the amount of energy for the mind and body to burn when compared to carbohydrates or sugar. As a side note, from another source (Google), based on 1,009 nights of data with fourteen chess players, their average amount of sleep was six hours and forty-four minutes with a standard deviation of one hour and thirty-five minutes.

Kasparov believes that each person, with their unique DNA, has a unique secret to success in life that will make them happy. The greatest predecessors and titans who contributed to his development were Alexander Alekhine and Winston Churchill. They taught him the virtue of fortitude: Never quit—never, never, never. Kasparov also believes that the goal in the journey of chess is about self-awareness and challenge. From his earliest memories at the age of six, Kasparov was always interested in maps, geography, travel, and adventures, and chess enabled him to travel the world and have adventures like Marco Polo, Columbus, and Magellan.

> Better decision making cannot be taught, but it can be self-taught. The secret is to pursue these challenges (decisive moments, turning points, forks in the road that define our lives) instead of avoiding them and quitting. This is the only way to discover, exploit, capitalize and benefit on all of our gifts. Developing our own personal blueprint with hard work allows us to make better decisions, to have confidence, to trust our instincts and to know that no matter what the result, we will come out stronger which

is our unique secret of success in life which will make us happy. (Kasparov)

Therefore, Kasparov believes the secret to success in life is to work hard and to never quit (*How Life Imitates Chess: Insights into Life as a Game of Strategy*, Garry Kasparov).

1

Kasparov as the Inspiring Coach

Garry Kasparov inspired and empowered me with my first series of lessons in chess on my birthday, and through the MasterClass series, he initiated a lifelong journey in the pursuit of happiness. I was familiar with Garry at a much earlier time, some thirty-five years ago, in the 1980s, which defined me as a person with my progression from youth to adult. The decade of the 1980s was the most impactful and profound decade in my life. The world was a very different place, and Garry stood out as an icon of intellect and the ultimate chess achievement as world champion. He dominated the chess world with his aggressive, big, bold, and dynamic style, which also made him an international celebrity. I am a product of the 1980s and the Garry Kasparov chess era.

A brilliant description of happiness hails from the nineteenth century and the famous Siegbert Tarrasch quote: "Chess, like love, like music, has the power to make men happy." Playing chess will enable you to find happiness with new and creative answers and solutions in your everyday life as an endless process of exploration in life's journey. Additional happiness can be derived from contributing knowledge to an institution that is greater than you as well as being able to go to war and kill without death and destruction.

The true purpose of this book is to help inspire, uplift, motivate, and magnify your love for chess—the greatest game in the world—past, present, and future. I hope you will play chess and find happiness for the rest of your life. This book was written by a beginner for a beginner.

2

King's Bunker Strategy:
The Best Offense Is a Better Defense

Challenge

Chess is a two-dimensional game and was originally designed with the king/queen or top civilian-political and military leader going into battle with his/her army in a two-dimensional landscape. However, we live in a three-dimensional world where the top civilian-political and military leaders do not go to the battlefield with their armies because they remain in a bunker or bunkers. The United States uses Mount Weather for its top civilian-political leaders and Raven Rock for its top military leaders.

- Modern Thesis: The best defense is a good offense.
- Hypermodern Thesis: The best offense is a better defense.

In the two-dimensional, medieval, fifteenth-century cavalry battlefield, the king is engaged on the battlefield, and a limited amount of security can be provided to the most valuable asset in the entire kingdom. However, we live in a three-dimensional, modern, twentieth-century mechanized battlefield where the top civilian-political and military leaders command from bunkers in the most secure locations on the battlefields to ensure their survival and eventual victory.

Solution

Place the king in his bunker as soon as possible, and as a rule, keep him there to ensure a better defense than the opponent's defense, thereby denying the enemy of relative increased opportunities to checkmate your king and win.

Unique Point of This Book

When you deploy a three-dimensional defensive structure on a two-dimensional battlefield, you increase the value of the defense's fortification by an approximate factor of three, thereby doubling the probability of a victory. Applying a technology of a higher dimension to a lower dimension creates a force multiplier effect of an ancient mystery, which greatly enhances the capabilities of the lower dimension.

Rule

After castling on the fourth move, maintain the king in the King's Bunker Strategy/Position with the following positions: pawn on f2, pawn on g2, pawn on h2, rook on f1, king on g1, and nothing on h1.

Methodology

I played five hundred chess games with two openings, King's Pawn Opening and the Reti Opening, and I castled on the fourth move. As with most beginners, I always played white.

As a final note of caution, there may be a certain amount of psychosis that can result from playing too much chess. We live in a three-dimensional world and spending too much time in a two-dimensional world affects the subconscious and prevents us from maintaining equilibrium. We can lose touch with reality. Physicists who spend too much time in higher dimensions seeking parallel universes with a gravitino 3/2 spin or a graviton 2/2 spin are subject to psychosis because our brains have not yet evolved to a level to manage such sustained illumination. A current research article on arXiv.org suggests that the high-energy universe could have just the right conditions to populate the universe with gravitinos.

Therefore, as with all passions, temperance must always be observed.

Introduction Mantra: Play Chess. Be Happy.

Herewith, I am submitting the most significant eighty games of the five hundred games I played in three categories: "Bunker Busted and Won," "Bunker Busted and Lost," and "Draw."

3

Bunker Busted and Won: Fifty Games

Game 1

1. e4 e6 2. Bc4 Bb4 3. Nf3 Bf8 4. 0-0 a6 5. Bb3 a5 6. d4 Bd6 7. e5 Bf8 8. d5 a4 9. Bc4 c6 10. d6 Ra5 11. Qd4 b5 12. Be2 Na6 13. Bd2 Bb7 14. b4 Nxb4 15. Qxb4 Ra8 16. c4 Nh6 17. cxb5 Rb8 18. Nc3 Ra8 19. b6 a3 20. Ne4 Ng4 21. Nc5 Qc8 22. Qxg4 g6 23. Qg5 h6 24. Qf6 Rh7 25. Bxh6 Rxh6 26. Ng5 Rxh2 27. Qxf7+ Kd8 28. Qxf8#

Notes

Game 2

1. e4 e6 2. Bc4 e5 3. Nf3 Bd6 4. 0-0 Qf6 5. Nc3 a6 6. Nd5 Qg6 7. d4 b6
8. dxe5 h6 9. exd6 Qxd6 10. Bf4 Qc6 11. Nxc7+ Kf8 12. Bd6+ Ne7 13.
Ne5 Qxe4 14. Bxe7+ Kxe7 15. Nxf7 Qxc4 16. Nxh8 Qxc7 17. Qd5 Ra7
18. Rae1+ Kf6 19. Qh5 Qxh2+ 20. Kxh2 a5 21. Qg6#

Notes

Game 3

1. e4 c5 2. Bc4 g6 3. Nf3 e6 4. 0-0 Nh6 5. d3 b6 6. Nc3 Ng4 7. Bf4 Na6
8. Nb5 d6 9. d4 Be7 10. dxc5 d5 11. exd5 Bxc5 12. dxe6 fxe6 13. Nd6+
Kf8 14. Ng5 Nxf2 15. Rxf2 Bxf2+ 16. Kxf2 Nc5 17. Qd4 Kg8 18. Ngf7
Ne4+ 19. Ke3 Qf6 20. Qxe4 a6 21. Qxa8 Qxf7 22. Qxc8+ Qf8 23. Qxe6+
Kg7 24. Qd7+ Kf6 25. e4#

Notes

Game 4

1. Nf3 Nf6 2. e4 Nh5 3. Bc4 Nf6 4. 0-0 b5 5. Bd3 b4 6. e5 Ng8 7. a3 h6
8. axb4 e6 9. c3 h5 10. Be4 Nc6 11. b5 g5 12. d4 d5 13. exd6 Nxd4 14.
Qxd4 Bxd6 15. Qxh8 Bxh2+ 16. Kxh2 Qd6+ 17. Ne5 Bb7 18. Bxb7 f6
19. Qxg8+ Ke7 20. Qf7+ Kd8 21. Rd1 Qxd1 22. Nc6#

Notes

Game 5

1. e4 c5 2. Nf3 e6 3. Bc4 g5 4. 0-0 d6 5. d4 g4 6. Ne1 Nd7 7. Be3 h5 8. dxc5 dxc5 9. Nd2 Nb6 10. Qe2 Rh7 11. Rd1 Be7 12. Nd3 a5 13. Bb5+ Kf8 14. Nb3 Nd5 15. exd5 e5 16. Nxe5 f6 17. d6 Bxd6 18. Rxd6 Qxd6 19. Bxc5 Qxc5 20. Ng6+ Kg7 21. Nxc5 Rb8 22. Qe8 h4 23. Qf8+ Kxg6 24. Be8+ Kg5 25. Qxg8+ Rg7 26. Qxg7+ Kf5 27. Nd3 h3 28. Bf7 Ke4 29. Qxf6 hxg2 30. Qf4#

Notes

Game 6

1. e4 c5 2. Nf3 Nc6 3. Bc4 e6 4. 0-0 Rb8 5. d4 h6 6. d5 e5 7. dxc6 Be7
8. Qd5 Qc7 9. Qxf7+ Kd8 10. Qxg7 bxc6 11. Nxe5 d5 12. Qxh8 Be6 13.
Nxc6+ Qxc6 14. exd5 Bxd5 15. Qe5 Bxc4 16. Qxb8+ Kd7 17. Qxa7+ Kc8
18. Bf4 Bd6 19. Bxd6 Bxf1 20. Qb8+ Kd7 21. Qxg8 Bxg2 22. Nc3 Qxd6
23. Rd1 Qxd1+ 24. Nxd1 Bb7 25. Ne3 Bf3 26. Qf7+ Kc6 27. Qxf3+ Kc7
28. Qd5 Kb8 29. Qxc5 Ka8 30. Nd5 Kb7 31. Qd6 h5 32. Qh6 Kc8 33.
Qxh5 Kb7 34. Qg6 Kb8 35. Qb6+ Ka8 36. c7#

Notes

Game 7

1. Nf3 Nf6 2. e4 b6 3. Bc4 d6 4. 0-0 h5 5. d4 e6 6. e5 Ng4 7. Qe2 d5 8. Bd3 a6 9. c4 Be7 10. Nc3 dxc4 11. Bxc4 h4 12. Qe4 h3 13. Qxa8 b5 14. Bxb5+ axb5 15. Qxb8 Kf8 16. a4 b4 17. Ne4 Rh5 18. Bg5 hxg2 19. Bxe7+ Kxe7 20. Qxb4+ c5 21. Qxc5+ Kd7 22. Rac1 gxf1=Q+ 23. Kxf1 Bb7 24. Qb5+ Ke7 25. Qxb7+ Qd7 26. Rc7 Nxh2+ 27. Nxh2 Qxc7 28. Qxc7+ Ke8 29. Nd6+ Kf8 30. Qxf7#

Notes

Game 8

1. e4 c5 2. Bc4 g6 3. Nf3 e6 4. 0-0 Nh6 5. d4 Qe7 6. Bg5 f6 7. Be3 cxd4
8. Nxd4 Nf7 9. Nb5 Nd6 10. Bc5 Nxc4 11. Nc7+ Kf7 12. Bxe7 Bxe7 13.
Nxa8 a5 14. Qe2 Nxb2 15. Nb6 a4 16. Qb5 a3 17. Qb3 Rd8 18. Nxa3 f5
19. e5 Bxa3 20. Qxa3 Nd3 21. cxd3 Nc6 22. Qd6 Ne7 23. Rac1 f4 24.
Nxc8 Rxc8 25. Rxc8 Nxc8 26. Qxd7+ Ne7 27. Qxb7 Kf8 28. Qd7 Kf7
29. Qb7 Kf8 30. a4 h5 31. a5 Kf7 32. a6 g5 33. a7 g4 34. a8=Q f3 35.
Qh8 fxg2 36. Qh7+ Kf8 37. Qbxe7#

Notes

Game 9

1. Nf3 e6 2. e4 d5 3. Bc4 dxc4 4. 0-0 Bc5 5. Qe2 Nf6 6. Qxc4 Na6 7. d4
Bd6 8. e5 Nd7 9. exd6 cxd6 10. Bf4 Qe7 11. Qb3 Nab8 12. Nc3 0-0 13.
Qa3 Nc5 14. dxc5 dxc 5 15. Rad1 Kh8 16. Bxb8 g5 17. Bd6 Qd8 18. Be5+
Kg8 19. Rxd8 Rxd8 20. Qxc5 Bd7 21. Ne4 h6 22. Qe7 Bb5 23. Nf6+ Kh8
24. Qxf7 Bxf1 25. Qh7#

Notes

Game 10

1. Nf3 Nf6 2. e4 d6 3. Bc4 h5 4. 0-0 b6 5. d4 e6 6. e5 Ng4 7. Nc3 d5 8. Bd3 Bb7 9. a4 Be7 10. a5 Kd7 11. Bf4 Ke8 12. axb6 cxb6 13. Nb5 Nc6 14. c3 Kd7 15. Nd6 Qb8 16. Nxb7 Qxb7 17. c4 Rac8 18. cxd5 exd5 19. Ba6 Qb8 20. e6+ fxe6 21. Bxb8 Rxb8 22. Bb5 Kc7 23. Qc1 bc5 24. Qf4+ e5 25. Qf7+ Be7 26. Bxc6 Nxh2 27. Qxe7+ Kxc6 28. Nxe5+ Kb5 29. Qd7+ Kb4 30. Qa4#

Notes

Game 11

1. Nf3 Nf6 2. e4 a6 3. Bc4 c5 4. 0-0 h6 5. e5 Nh5 6. d4 b5 7. Bxf7+ Kxf7
8. Nh4 d5 9. Qxh5+ Kg8 10. a4 e6 11. axb5 c4 12. Nc3 a5 13. Bd2 Ra7
14. Ne2 Qb6 15. Nf4 a4 16. Qe8 Bb7 17. Nxe6 Nd7 18. Nf5 c3 19. Ne7+
Kh7 20. Qg6#

Notes

Game 12

1. e4 e5 2. Bc4 Nf6 3. Nf3 Qe7 4. 0-0 Na6 5. d4 exd4 6. Ng5 c5 7. e5 d5
8. exd6 Bg4 9. Bb5+ bd7 10. dxe7 Bxb5 11. exf8=Q+ Kxf8 12. Nd2 Nc7
13. Nde4 Rc8 14. Qf3 Bxf1 15. Nxf6 Bb5 16. Nd7+ Ke7 17. Qxf7+ Kd8
18. Nxc5 Rb8 19. Nge6+ Nxe6 20. Nxe6+ Kc8 21. Qc7#

Notes

Game 13

1. e4 e5 2. Bc4 Nf6 3. Nf3 Nc6 4. 0-0 Be7 5. d4 exd4 6. e5 Ng4 7. Qe2
a5 8. c3 Bc5 9. cxd4 Bb6 10. d5 Nb8 11. Bg5 0-0 12. Bxd8 Rxd8 13. Ng5
h5 14. d6 Rf8 15. Qe4 Bxf2+ 16. Rxf2 g6 17. Qxg6+ Kh8 18. Qh7#

Notes

Game 14

1. e4 c5 2. Bc4 g6 3. Nf3 a5 4. 0-0 f6 5. Nc3 Nc6 6. d4 cxd4 7. Nxd4 d6
8. Ne6 Qb6 9. Nd5 Bxe6 10. Nxb6 Bxc4 11. Nxa8 h5 12. Nc7+ Kf7 13.
b3 Bxf1 14. Qd5+ Kg7 15. Ne8+ Kh7 16. Qf7+ Bg7 17. Qxg7#

Notes

Game 15

1. Nf3 d5 2. e4 dxe4 3. Bc4 Qd6 4. 0-0 e6 5. Ng5 Qd4 6. d3 Nd7 7. Nc3 a6 8. Ncxe4 c5 9. Qh5 g6 10. Qh3 Ndf6 11. Nxf7 Kxf7 12. Bxe6+ Kg7 13. Bxc8 Nxe4 14. dxe4 Rxc8 15. Qxc8 Be7 16. Qc7 b5 17. e5 h5 18. Bg5 c4 19. Bxe7 Nxe7 20. Qxe7+ Kg8 21. Rad1 Qb6 22. Rd7 Qxf2+ 23. Rxf2 h4 24. Qe8#

Notes

Game 16

1. e4 c5 2. Bc4 e5 3. Bf3 d6 4. 0-0 g6 5. d4 exd4 6. c3 Nc6 7. cxd4 Qe7
8. dxc5 dxc5 9. Nc3 Be6 10. Nd5 Qd6 11. Bf4 Bxd5 12. Bxd6 Bxc4 13.
Bxf8 Kxf8 14. Qd6+ Kg7 15. Rac1 Be2 16. Ne5 Nce7 17. Rxc5 Re8 18.
Rc7 Bxf1 19. Kxf1 g5 20. Rxb7 a5 21. Qd4 Nf6 22. Nd7 Nd5 23. exd5
g4 24. Qxf6+ Kg8 25. Qg5#

Notes

Game 17

1. e4 e5 2. Bc4 Nf6 3. Nf3 Nc6 4. 0-0 h6 5. d4 a6 6. Nxe5 d5 7. exd5 Ne7
8. d6 Nfd5 9. dxe7 Bxe7 10. Nxf7 Kxf7 11. Qf3+ Bf6 12. Bxd5+ Kf8 13.
Bf4 a5 14. Bc4 Ra7 15. Qh5 Qe7 16. Bxc7 Ra8 17. Bd6 g6 18. Qxg6 Be6
19. Bxe7+ Kxe7 20. Qe4 Kf8 21. Qxb7 Bxc4 22. d5 Bxf1 23. Qxa8+ Kf7
24. Qb7+ Be7 25. d6 bb5 26. Nc3 Bc4 27. Qxe7+ Kg6 28. Qe4+ Kf7 29.
Qxc4+ Kf8 30. Re1 Kg7 31. Qg4+ Kf7 32. Re7+ Kf8 33. Qc8#

Notes

Game 18

1. Nf3 d6 2. e4 Nf6 3. Bc4 e6 4. 0-0 h6 5. e5 Nh5 6. d4 Na6 7. d5 c6 8. dxe6 fxe6 9. Nd4 Rb8 10. a4 Qh4 11. b4 dxe5 12. Nxe6 Bxb4 13. Bg5 hxg5 14. Nd2 Nf6 15. Nf3 Bxe6 16. Nxh4 Bxc4 17. Ng6 Bxf1 18. Nxh8 Bc4 19. Ng6 Nd7 20. Qg4 e4 21. Qxe4+ Be6 22. Qxe6+ Kd8 23. Rd1 Nc5 24. Qd6 Kc8 25. e5 Bd2 26. Rxd2 Ra8 27. Nxd7 Ne4 28. Nb6+ axb6 29. Qd8#

Notes

Game 19

1. Nf3 Nf6 2. e4 Nc6 3. Bc4 g6 4. 0-0 Nh5 5. e5 e6 6. d4 Bb4 7. d5 Na5
8. Be2 exd5 9. Qxd5 c5 10. a3 Ng3 11. Re1 Nxe2+ 12. Rxe2 Nc6 13. axb4
0-0 14. Re1 cxb4 15. Rf1 h5 16. Bg5 Qb6 17. Bf6 a5 18. Nbd2 Re8 19.
Nc4 Qa6 20. Ng5 Nxe5 21. Bxe5 Rf8 22. Nd6 Rb8 23. Ndxf7 Qxf1+ 24.
Kxf1 Rd8 25. Nxd8+ Kf8 26. Qf7#

Notes

Game 20

1. Nf3 Nf6 2. e4 Bc6 3. Bc4 Nh5 4. 0-0 f6 5. d4 e5 6. dxe5 fxe5 7. Nxe5
g6 8. Bf7+ Ke7 9. Qxh5 gxh5 10. Bg5+ Kd6 11. Bxd8 Kxe5 12. Bg5 Na5
13. Nc3 h6 14. Bxh6 Bd6 15. Nb5 Rxh6 16. Rad1 Kf4 17. Rd5 Be5 18.
Rd3 Nc6 19. a4 Ne7 20. b4 Rh7 21. c4 Rxf7 22. Rf3+ Kg5 23. Rxf7c6
24. Nxa7 Rxa7 25. Rxe7 d6 26. Re8 Bg4 27. Rg8+ Kh6 28. a5 Be2 29. c5
Bc3 30. cxd6 Bxf1 31. d7 Ra8 32. Rxa8 Bf6 33. e5 Bh4 34. Kxf1 Bd8 35.
Rxd8 Kg7 36. e6 Kh7 37. e7 b5 38. e8=Q Kh6 39. Qf7 Kg5 40. Rg8+
Kh6 41. d8=Q h4 42. Qxh4#

Notes

Game 21

1. Nf3 c5 2. e4 Nc6 3. Bc4 e6 4. 0-0 Bb4 5. Nc3 Ne7 6. d4 Nec6 7. d5 Na5 8. Bb5 c4 9. a3 Bc5 10. axb4 Bxf2+ 11. Rxf2 Bc6 12. dxc6 bxc6 13. Ng5 g6 14. Nxf7 Qc7 15. Nd6+ Ke7 16. Bg5#

Notes

Game 22

1. e4 e6 2. Bb5 c6 3. Nf3 Qb6 4. 0-0 cxb5 5. a4 a6 6. d3 Ra7 7. Be3 Bc5
8. d4 f6 9. dxc5 Qa5 10. c3 h6 11. b4 Qc7 12. axb5 Qd8 13. Qd6 Ra8 14.
Nbd2 g5 15. Nc4 Kf7 16. Nb6 g4 17. Nd2 Rh7 18. Nxa8 axb5 19. Qxb8
e5 20. Nc7 Kg7 21. Nxb5 Rh8 22. Nd6 Ne7 23. Ra8 g3 24. Nxc8 gxh2+
25. Kxh2 Nxc8 26. Qxb7 Re8 27. c6 Kg8 28. cxd7 Rf8 29. dxc8=Q Qxc8
30. Rxc8 Rxc8 31. Bxh6 Rc7 32. Qxc7 Kh8 33. Qg7#

Notes

Game 23

1. Nf3 Nf6 2. e4 e5 3. Bc4 c6 4. 0-0 d5 5. Bb3 Qa5 6. Nxe5 Bd6 7. d4
0-0 8. exd5 c5 9. Nc4 Bxh2+ 10. Kxh2 Qb5 11. Nc3 Qd7 12. Kg1 Rd8
13. dxc5 Qf5 14. Re1 h6 15. Nd6 Qd7 16. Nxf7 Kxf7 17. c6 Qf5 18. d6+
Kg6 19. cxb7 Bxb7 20. Be6 Qc5 21. Qd3+ Ne4 22. Nxe4 Qc6 23. Ng5+
Kh5 24. Bf7+ Kg4 25. Qh3#

Notes

Game 24

1. e4 e5 2. Bc4 Nf6 3. Nf3 Qe7 4. 0-0 Na6 5. d4 d5 6. Bxa6 Qd6 7. Bb5+
c6 8. dxe5 Qc5 9. exf6 cxb5 10. exd5 Kd8 11. Ng5 b4 12. Nxf7+ Kc7
13. Bf4+ Kb6 14. Be3 Qxe3 15. fxe3 Rg8 16. d6 Ka6 17. Qd3+ b5 18. a4
Bd7 19. axb5+ Kb6 20. Qd4+ Kb7 21. Qd5+ Kb8 22. Nd8 Bc8 23. Qc6
gxf6 24. Qc7#

Notes

Game 25

1. Nf3 Nf6 2. e4 h6 3. Bc4 Na6 4. 0-0 h5 5. e5 Nc5 6. exf6 gxf6 7. Nc3
Rg8 8. d4 Ne6 9. d5 Nf4 10. Bxf4 b6 11. d6 cxd6 12. Qd5 e6 13. Qxa8
Qc7 14. Bd3 e5 15. Bd5 Qd8 16. Qxa7 f5 17. Be3 Rg6 18. Bxb6 Rxg2+
19. Kxg2 f4 20. Bxd8 f5 21. Qc7 Bg7 22. Qxd6 Bf8 23. Qg6+ Kxd8 24.
Qf6+ Ke8 25. Nc7#

Notes

Game 26

1. e4 e5 2. Bc4 Nf6 3. Nf3 Ng4 4. 0-0 Nc6 5. Nc3 Bc5 6. Nd5 a5 7. c3
Rb8 8. d4 exd4 9. cxd4 Ba7 10. e5 0-0 11. Bg5 Qe8 12. Nxc7 Qd8 13.
Bxd8 Rxd8 14. Bxf7+ Kh8 15. Ng5 d6 16. Qd3 g6 17. Qh3 Nf6 18. Be6
Nxe5 19. dxe5 dxe5 20. Nf7+ Kg7 21. Qh6+ Kg8 22. Nxd8+ Bxe6 23.
Ncxe6 Bxf2+ 24. Rxf2 a4 25. Qg7#

Notes

Game 27

1. e4 e5 2. Bc4 Nf6 3. Nf3 Nc6 4. 0-0 Rg8 5. d4 exd4 6. Ng5 Be7 7. Bxf7+ Kf8 8. Bb3 Bd6 9. c3 b6 10. cxd4 Rh8 11. e5 Nxe5 12. dxe5 Bxe5 13. Ne6+ Ke7 14. Nxd8 Kxd8 15. Nc3 Ba6+ 16. Bg5 Re8 17. Bxf6+ Bxf6 18. Qf3 Rb8 19. Rae1 Rxe1 20. Rxe1 Bb7 21. Bf7 Be5 22. Rxe5 d6 23. Re8+ Kd7 24. Qf5+ Kc6 25. Qb5#

Notes

Game 28

1. Nf3 Nf6 2. e4 Nxe4 3. Bc4 Nf6 4. 0-0 b6 5. d4 a6 6. d5 g6 7. Nc3 a5
8. d6 cxd6 9. Bg5 Ra7 10. Bxf6 Rg8 11. Ng5 d5 12. Bxd5 Bh6 13. Nxf7
Qc7 14. Bxe7 Bf4 15. Nb5 Bxh2+ 16. Qh1 Ba6 17. Re1 Bxb5 18. Bd6+
Be2 19. Rxe2+ Be5 20. Rxe5#

Notes

Game 29

1. Nf3 Nf6 2. e4 a6 3. Bc4 e6 4. 0-0 Ng8 5. d4 h6 6. Bd3 g5 7. Be3 Nf6
8. c4 b6 9. e5 Ng4 10. Bd2 Bg7 11. Be4 Nc6 12. Nc3 Ra7 13. Bxc6 a5
14. Be4 Ba6 15. Na3 Qb8 16. Bc2 Ke7 17. d5 Qb7 18. dxe6 fxe6 19. Qd3
Rf8 20. Qg6 Rf7 21. Be4 Qb8 22. Rad1 Bh8 23. Rxd7+ Kxd7 24. Qxf7+
Kd8 25. Qf8+ Kd7 26. Qxb8 Ne3 27. Qxa7 Nxf1 28. Qxa6 Ne3 29. Qa8
Nxc4 30. Bc6+ Ke7 31. Qe8#

Notes

Game 30

1. Nf3 Nf6 2. e4 Nxe4 3. Bc4 c6 4. 0-0 e6 5. d4 Qf6 6. Bd3 Qf5 7. Ne5 Kd8 8. Bxe4 Qxe4 9. Nxf7+ Kc7 10. Nc3 Qg6 11. Nxh8 Qf5 12. Qd3 d5 13. Qxf5 exf5 14. Nf7 Bb4 15. Bf4+ Kd7 16. Rae1 a6 17. Na4 Bxe1 18. Rxe1 c5 19. Nb6+ Kc6 20. Nxa8 g5 21. Bxb8 g4 22. Ne5+ Kb5 23. a4+ Kb4 24. Nd3+ Ka5 25. b3 b6 26. Bc7 cxd4 27. Bxb6#

Notes

Game 31

1. e4 e5 2. Bc4 Nf6 3. Nf3 Nc6 4. 0-0 Bd6 5. c3 Nb8 6. d4 Qe7 7. Ng5 Qf8 8. Nxf7 b5 9. Bb3 exd4 10. Nxh8 Bxh2+ 11. Kxh2 dxc3 12. Nxc3 Qc5 13. Nd5 Ba6 14. Be3 Qc6 15. Rc1 Qd6+ 16. Bf4 Qf8 17. Nxc7+ Qd8 18. Ne6+ Ke8 19. Nxf8 Nc6 20. Bf7+ Kxf8 21. Qd6+ Ne7 22. e5 h6 23. exf6 Re8 24. fxg7+ Kxg7 25. Qxh6#

Notes

Game 32

1. Nf3 c5 2. e4 d6 3. Bc4 a6 4. 0-0 Qa5 5. c3 h6 6. d4 Nc6 7. Be3 Qc7 8. dxc5 g6 9. Nbd2 Qd8 10. cxd6 exd6 11. Qb3 Qd7 12. Bd5 b5 13. Nd4 Na5 14. Qb4 Nc4 15. Nxc4 Rb8 16. Bc6 Nf6 17. Nxd6+ Bxd6 18. Qxd6 h5 19. Qe5+ Kd8 20. Bxd7 Bxd7 21. Qxb8+ Ke7 22. Nf5+ gxf5 23. Qxh8 fxe4 24. Bg5 Bg4 25. Qxf6+ Kd7 26. Qxf7+ Kc6 27. Rad1 e3 28. Bd8 exf2+ 29. Kxf2 Bxd1 30. Rxd1 Kc5 31. Qd5#

Notes

Game 33

1. e4 c5 2. Bc4 h5 3. Nf3 g6 4. 0-0 Nf6 5. d4 Nxe4 6. dxc5 Nxc5 7. Qd4 d6 8. Qxh8 Nbd7 9. Bh6 b6 10. Bxf7+ Kxf7 11. Qh7+ Kf6 12. Bg5+ Kf5 13. Qf7+ Nf6 14. Bxf6 exf6 15. Qd5+ Kf4 16. Qxa8 a5 17. Nc3 Kg4 18. Nd5 h4 19. Nxb6 Qxb6 20. Qxc8+ f5 21. Qxf8 Qa6 22. Qh6 Qxf1+ 23. Rxf1 a4 24. Qxh4#

Notes

Game 34

1. e4 d6 2. Bc4 Nh6 3. Nf3 c6 4. 0-0 Bg4 5. d4 Qd7 6. Nc3 Rg8 7. a4
Na6 8. Bg5 Nb8 9. d5 Rh8 10. Qd3 a5 11. Rad1 Qd8 12. e5 Bf5 13. Qe2
b6 14. dxc6 Qc7 15. exd6 Qxc6 16. dxe7 Nd7 17. Nb5 Be6 18. Bxe6 fxe6
19. Nfd4 Qxg2+ 20. Kxg2 Bxe7 21. Qxe6 Ng8 22. Nc6 Ra6 23. Nd6+
Kf8 24. Qf7#

Notes

Game 35

1. Nf3 d5 2. e4 d4 3. Bc4 f6 4. 0-0 e5 5. d3 g6 6. c3 Qd7 7. cxd4 exd4 8. Qb3 Qg7 9. Nxd4 g5 10. Ne6 Bxe6 11. Qxb7 c6 12. Qxa8 Qc7 13. Bxe6 Bh6 14. Be3 a6 15. Ba7 a5 16. Qxb8+ Qxb8 17. Bxb8 c5 18. Bc3 Ke7 19. Bc4 Bf8 20. e5 f5 21. Bd6+ Kd7 22. Bxf8 a4 23. e6+ Kc8 24. Bg7 h6 25. Bxh8 Kb7 26. Bd5+ ka7 27. Nxa4 Ne7 28. Bc4 Ng6 29. Bf6 Nf4 30. e7 Ne2+ 31. Kh1 Ng3+ 32. Kg1 Ne2+ 33. Kh1 Ng3+ 34. fxg3 g4 35. e8=Q f4 36. Rfe1 fxg3 37. Re7#

Notes

Game 36

1. e4 c5 2. Bc4 Na6 3. Nf3 Nh6 4. 0-0 e6 5. d4 f6 6. Bxh6 Nc7 7. Bf4 b5
8. Be2 d6 9. dxc5 d5 10. Nc3 Bxc5 11. exd5 Kf7 12. d6 Na6 13. Bxb5 Bb7
14. Qe2 Nb8 15. Rae1 e5 16. Nxe5+ Kf8 17. Nf7 Bxf2+ 18. Rxf2 Kxf7
19. Qh5+ g6 20. Bc4+ Bd5 21. Qxd5+ Kf8 22. Qf7#

Notes

Game 37

1. Nf3 d5 2. e4 f5 3. Bc4 Nf6 4. 0-0 dxc4 5. e5 Ne4 6. d3 Nxf2 7. Rxf2 a6 8. Be3 b6 9. e6 Ra7 10. Ng5 Qd5 11. Nc3 Qa5 12. dxc4 Bb7 13. Rd2 Nc6 14. Rd8+ Nxd8 15. Qd7#

Notes

Game 38

1. e4 c5 2. Bc4 Nc6 3. Nf3 h5 4. 0-0 a5 5. d4 d5 6. exd5 Nh6 7. dxc6 e5
8. Nxe5 cxd4 9. Bxh6 Rxh6 10. Bxf7+ Ke7 11. Qf3 Rf6 12. cxb7 Rxf3
13. Bxa8=Q Rxf7 14. Nc6+ Kd7 15. Nxd8 Kxd8 16. Qd5+ Bd7 17. Qxf7
Bd6 18. Qxg7 Kc8 19. Qh8+ Kb7 20. Qxd4 Bxh2+ 21. Kxh2 Bg4 22. Re1
Kc6 23. Re7 Kb5 24. Nc3+ Kc6 25. Qd5+ Kb6 26. Qd6#

Notes

Game 39

1. e4 e5 2. Bc4 Nf6 3. Nf3 Qe7 4. 0-0 c6 5. d4 d5 6. exd5 Bg4 7. dxe5
Ng8 8. d6 Bxf3 9. Qxf3 Qd7 10. e6 fxe6 11. Bg5 Qxd6 12. Nd2 Na6 13.
Rad1 Nh6 14. Bxh6 Nc5 15. Ne4 Nxe4 16. Rxd6 Nxd6 17. Qh5+ kd7
18. Bf4 Be7 19. Bxd6 Bxd6 20. Qf7+ Kc8 21. Bxe6+ Kb8 22. Qxg7 Rf8
23. a4 c5 24. c4 b5 25. axb5 Re8 26. Qd7 Rxe6 27. Qxe6 Bc7 28. Qe8+
Kb7 29. Qc6+ Kb8 30. b4 h5 31. bxc5 Bd8 32. Qd7 Bh4 33. c6 Bxf2+
34. Rxf2 h4 35. Qb7#

Notes

Game 40

1. Nf3 Nf6 2. e4 Na6 3. Bc4 Rb8 4. 0-0 b6 5. e5 Ng4 6. Bxf7+ Kxf7 7.
Ng5+ Kg8 8. Qxg4 e6 9. d4 Ra8 10. Qf3 Qe7 11. Qxa8 c6 12. Qxc8 g6
13. Ne4 Nb4 14. Bg5 Qf7 15. Nf6+ Kg7 16. Ne8+ Kg8 17. Nd6 Qg7 18.
Bf6 Qh6 19. Qxd7 Bxd6 20. Qxe6+ Kf8 21. Qxd6+ Kf7 22. Bxh8 a5 23.
Nc3 Qf4 24. Qd7+ Kf8 25. e6 Qxh2+ 26. Kxh2 Nxc2 27. Qf7#

Notes

Game 41

1. Nf3 Nf6 2. e4 Na6 3. Bc4 Rb8 4. 0-0 b6 5. e5 Bg4 6. Nc3 e6 7. d4 Bb7
8. a3 Rg8 9. Qd3 Qc8 10. Qxh7 Nh6 11. Bxh6 Qd8 12. Bg5 Qc8 13. d5
exd5 14. Bxa6 Bxa6 15. Qxg8 Qb7 16. Nd4 Qa8 17. Nf5 d6 18. Nxg7+
Kd7 19. Qxf7+ Kc8 20. Ne6 Qc6 21. Nd8 Qd7 22. Qxf8 Ra8 23. e6 Qh7
24. e7 Bxf1 25. e8=Q a6 26. Nc6+ Kb7 27. Qxa8#

Notes

Game 42

1. e4 e5 2. Bc4 Bf6 3. Nf3 Bd6 4. 0-0 0-0 5. d4 Qe7 6. c3 exd4 7. cxd4 h5 8. Bg5 Qxe4 9. Bd3 Qc6 10. Bxf6 gxf6 11. Nh4 Qd5 12. Nf5 Rd8 13. Qxh5 c6 14. Qg4+ Kf8 15. Qg7+ Ke8 16. Qg8+ Bf8 17. Nc3 Qe6 18. Ng7+ Ke7 19. Nxe6 dxe6 20. Rad1 Bh6 21. Qh7 Bf4 22. Bg6 a6 23. Qxf7+ Kd6 24. Ne4+ Kd5 25. Qe7 Bxh2+ 26. Kxh2 f5 27. Qc5+ Kxe4 28. Qe5#

Notes

Game 43

1. Nf3 g6 2. e4 Bg7 3. Bc4 b6 4. 0-0 h5 5. Qe2 c6 6. d4 Bf8 7. Nc3 a6 8.
Ne5 e6 9. Qf3 Nh6 10. Bxh6 Qe7 11. Bg5 f6 12. Bxf6 Qh7 13. Na4 b5
14. Bb6 Bb7 15. Bxh8 bxc4 16. Nexc4 Qxh8 17. Nxa8 Bxa8 18. Qb3 Bb7
19. Qxb7 Be7 20. Qxb8+ Bd8 21. Nd6+ Ke7 22. e5 g5 23. Nc4 Kf7 24.
Qb7 Be7 25. Qxd7 Qg7 26. Nd6+ Kg8 27. Qxe6+ Kh8 28. Nf5 Qh7 29.
Qc8+ Qg8 30. Qxg8+ Kxg8 31. Nxe7+ Kg7 32. Nxc6 g4 33. e6 Kf8 34.
d5 h4 35. d6 Ke8 36. d7+ Kf8 37. d8=Q+ Kg7 38. Qg5+ Kh7 39. e7 h3
40. e8=Q hxg2 41. Qeh5#

Notes

Game 44

1. e4 e5 2. Bc4 Nf6 3. Nf3 Nc6 4. 0-0 Rg8 5. d4 exd4 6. Ng5 Ne5 7. Bb3 c5 8. Nd2 a5 9. Nc4 Qe7 10. Nxe5 Qxe5 11. Bxf7+ Ke7 12. Bxg8 d6 13. Bb3 Ra7 14. Qd3 Ra6 15. Bc4 Rc6 16. Bd2 Bd7 17. Rae1 a4 18. Nf3 Qh5 19. e5 Ng4 20. Bg5+ Qxg5 21. exd6+ Kd8 22. Nxg5 Bxd6 23. Nf7+ Kc7 24. Nxd6 Rxd6 25. Re7 Ne3 26. Rxd7+ Rxd7 27. Bb5 Rd5 28. Qe4 Rf5 29. Qe7+ Kb6 30. Bxa4 Nxf1 31. Qe6+ Ka5 32. Qxf5 Nxh2 33. Qxc5+ Kxa4 34. b3#

Notes

Game 45

1. Nf3 Nf6 2. e4 e6 3. Bc4 h5 4. 0-0 Rh6 5. d4 Rg6 6. Ne5 Qe7 7. Nc3
Rg4 8. Nxg4 Nxg4 9. Bf4 g6 10. Bxc7 g5 11. Nb5 Nxf2 12. Rxf2 Qb4
13. Qxh5 Qe7 14. Nd6+ Qxd6 15. Qxf7#

Notes

Game 46

1. Nf3 d5 2. e4 dxe4 3. Bc4 Bf5 4. 0-0 Bg6 5. Nh4 Qd4 6. Na3 c6 7. c3
Qc5 8. Nxg6 fxg6 9. Qb3 Qb6 10. Bf7+ Kd8 11. Bxg8 h5 12. Qf7 Nd7
13. d3 exd3 14. Nc4 Qb5 15. Bf4 h4 16. Ne5 Nxe5 17. Qxf8+ Kc7 18.
Qxa8 Qc5 19. Rae1 Rh5 20. Rxe5 Rxe5 21. Bxe5+ Qxe5 22. Qxa7 Qh5
23. Qe3 Qe2 24. Qxe2 dxe2 25. a4 exf1=Q+ 26. Kxf1 Kd7 27. Bh7 g5
28. a5 Ke8 29. b4 Kd7 30. Bf5+ Kd6 31. c4 e6 32. Bh3 Ke5 33. b5c5 34.
a6 b6 35. a7 g6 36. a8=Q Kd4 37. Bxe6 Kc3 38. Qa3+ Kc2 39. Ke2 Kb1
40. Bd5 Kc2 41. Be4#

Notes

Game 47

1. Nf3 Nf6 2. e4 c5 3. Bc4 e6 4. 0-0 Qb6 5. d3 Nc6 6. Nc3 Qd8 7. Bf4
Qb6 8. Nb5 Ke7 9. Ng5 Na5 10. Bd6+ Ke8 11. Nc7+ Qxc7 12. Bxc7 b6
13. e5 Nxc4 14. Qf3 h6 15. Qxa8 Nxe5 16. Nf3 Nxf3+ 17. Kh1 Nd2 18.
Qxa7 Nd5 19. a4 Nxf1 20. Qb8 Nxc7 21. Qxc8+ Ke7 22. Qxc7 Nd2 23.
Qxb6 h5 24. a5 g6 25. a6 Rg8 26. a7 Bh6 27. a8=Q Rxa8 28. Rxa8 Nf1
29. Qxc5+ Kf6 30. b4 g5 31. b5 h4 32. b6 h3 33. Qd4+ e5 34. Qd6+ Kg7
35. Qxe5+ Kg6 36. Rg8+ Kh5 37. Qe2+ Kh4 38. Qe4+ Kh5 39. Qf3+
Kh4 40. Qxh3#

Notes

Game 48

1. e4 e5 2. Nf3 Nc6 3. Bc4 Bc5 4. 0-0 d6 5. c3 Nf6 6. d4 g6 7. dxc5 Ke7
8. Bg5 Rg8 9. Nbd2 dxc5 10. Qb3 h6 11. Bxh6 Qe8 12. Ng5 Ng4 13.
Bxf7 Nxh6 14. Bxe8 Kxe8 15. Qd5 Ke7 16. Nc4 Rd8 17. Qxc5+ Rd6 18.
Nxe5 a5 19. Nxc6+ bxc6 20. e5 Nf7 21. exd6+ cxd6 22. Qxc6 Nxg5 23.
Rae1+ Kf6 24. Qxa8 Nf3+ 25. Kh1 Nxe1 26. Qxa5 Nd3 27. Qd8+ Ke5 28.
Qh8+ Kf5 29. b4 g5 30. b5 Ne5 31. a4 Bb7 32. a5 Ng6 33. Qh7 Bd5 34.
b6 Kf6 35. b7 Bxg2+ 36. Kxg2 Nf4+ 37. Kf3 g4+ 38. Kxf4 g3 39. b8=Q
Ke6 40. Re1+ Kf6 41. Qxd6#

Notes

Game 49

1. Nf3 d5 2. e4 dxe4 3. Bc4 c6 4. 0-0 a5 5. Bg5 e6 6. Nxe4 Ra7 7. d4 Qc7
8. Qf3 Ra8 9. Bf4 Qb6 10. Nbd2 Qb4 11. Qg3 Qxb3 12. Bxb8 Qxd4 13.
Be5 Qd8 14. Bxg7 b6 15. Bxh8 Qe7 16. Qxg8 Kd8 17. Bf6 Kc7 18. Be5+
Kd8 19. Nf3 Bb7 20. Rad1+ Kc8 21. Nd6+ Kb8 22. Nf5+ Ka7 23. Bb8+
Rxb8 24. N5h4 h5 25. Ne5 Qxh4 26. Qxf7 Qe7 27. Qxh5 Qf6 28. Nd7
Qe7 29. Qe5 Rd8 30. Nxb6 c5 31. Qc3 Re8 32. Nd7 Ba6 33. Qxa5 Kb7
34. Qa4 Kc7 35. Bxe6 Qxe6 36. Nf6 Re7 37. Nd5+ Kc8 38. Rb1 Qxd5 39.
Qg4+ Re6 40. Rb6 Bxf1 41. Rxe6 Kc7 42. Kxf1 Bd6 43. a4 Kb7 44. c4
Qd3+ 45. Qe2 Qb1+ 46. Qe1 Qb6 47. Qd1 Kc7 48. Rh6 Qa6 49. Rh7+
Kc8 50. Qd5 Qb6 51. Qe6+ Kb8 52. Qe8+ Qd8 53. Qxd8#

Notes

Game 50

1. Nf3 Nf6 2. e4 g6 3. Bc4 d6 4. 0-0 a5 5. e5 Ng4 6. d4 c6 7. exd6 Rg8
8. dxe7 Qxe7 9. Ng5 Rg7 10. Bf4 h5 11. Nc3 Kd8 12. d5 Ke8 13. dxc6
Nxc6 14. Nd5 Nxf2 15. Rxf2 Bg4 16. Qf1 Bf5 17. Re1 Qxe1 18. Qxe1+
Kd8 19. Nf6 Bd6 20. Qe8+ Kc7 21. Nd5#

Notes

4

Bunker Busted and Lost: Twenty-Five Games

Game 1

1. Nf3 Nf6 2. e4 b6 3. Bc4 Rg8 4. 0-0 g6 5. Nc3 h6 6. e5 Nh5 7. Qe2 Bb7 8. d4 Rh8 9. d5 Rh7 10. e6 Nf6 11. Ne5 dxe6 12. Bb5+ Nbd7 13. Nxd7 Nxd7 14. dxe6 fxe6 15. Qxe6 Rg7 16. Bxh6 c6 17. Bxg7 Bxg7 18. Qg8+ Nf8 19. Qxg7 cxb5 20. Rad1 Qc8 21. Nxb5 Qc4 22. Rde1 0-0-0 23. Rxe7 Qd5 24. Nxa7+ Kb8 25. a4 Qxg2#

Notes

Game 2

1. e4 c5 2. Bc4 g6 3. Nf3 h6 4. 0-0 d6 5. Ne5 Rh7 6. d4 a6 7. Bxf7+ Rxf7
8. Nxf7 Qd7 9. d5 b6 10. e5 a5 11. b4 Kxf7 12. bxa5 bxa5 13. e6+ Qxe6
14. a4 Qf6 15. Ra3 e6 16. dxe6+ Bxe6 17. Qxd6 Bxd6 18. Nc3 Ra6 19.
Bb5 Be7 20. Nc7 Qf5 21. Nxa6 Nxa6 22. Bxh6 Bd7 23. Rb3 Bf6 24. Rb8
Nxb8 25. Bf8 Qh5 26. Bd6 Nc6 27. Bc7 Qh8 28. Bb6 Kf8 29. Bxc5+ Kg7
30. c4 Nd4 31. Bd6 Qh5 32. Bc7 Ne7 33. c5 Ne2+ 34. Kh1 Qxc5 35. Bd8
Bxa4 36. Bxe7 Bxe7 37. Re1 Qc4 38. Rf1 Bc6 39. Rb1 Qd3 40. Re1 Bd8
41. Rf1 Bg5 42. Ra1 Qd5 43. Rg1 Nxg1 44. Kxg1 Qxg2#

Notes

Game 3

1. e4 e5 2. Bc4 Nf6 3. Nf3 Bd6 4. 0-0 h6 5. d4 h5 6. Nc3 exd4 7. Bf4 dxc3 8. bxc3 Bxf4 9. Ne5 Bxe5 10. Qd3 0-0 11. Rae1 Ng4 12. Qd5 g6 13. Qxe5 Nxe5 14. Bd5 c6 15. Bb3 Kh7 16. c4 Ng4 17. a4 a5 18. c5 Na6 19. c4 Nxc5 20. e5 Nxb3 21. e6 fxe6 22. c5 Qc7 23. Re5 Qxe5 24. Re1 Qxe1#

Notes

Game 4

1. e4 e6 2. Bc4 b6 3. Nf3 c5 4. 0-0 Ke7 5. a4 Ke8 6. d3 Bd6 7. Bf4 Bxf4
8. Nc3 d6 9. a5 Nh6 10. axb6 Qxb6 11. Ne5 Bxe5 12. Nd5 exd5 13. Bxd5
Bg4 14. Qe1 Nc6 15. c4 f6 16. b4 cxb4 17. Rxa7 Rxa7 18. Qa1 Rxa1 19.
c5 Rxf1+ 20. Kxf1 Qxc5 21. Bxc6+ Qxc6 22. d4 Qc1#

Notes

Game 5

1. e4 e5 2. Bc4 Nf6 3. Nf3 Bc5 4. 0-0 Kf8 5. a4 Na6 6. c3 Ng4 7. d4 Rg8
8. Be3 Nxe3 9. Nbd2 Nxd1 10. Raxd1 Bb6 11. b4 exd4 12. cxd4 Rb8 13.
Bxa6 h6 14. a5 Bxd4 15. Bxd4 d6 16. Be2 Ke8 17. b5 Qd7 18. Bc4 Rf8 19.
Bh5 Rg8 20. Bxf7+ Kxf7 21. e5 h5 22. exd6 Re8 23. Nf5 Ra8 24. dxc7
Qxf5 25. Nd6+ Kg6 26. Nxf5 Bxf5 27. b6 Bc2 28. Rd6+ Kf7 29. a6 g6
30. axb7 axb6 31. bxa8=Q Rxa8 32. c8=Q Rxc8 33. Rxb6 Rc7 34. Rf6+
Kxf6 35. Rc1 Ke5 36. Rxc2 Rxc2 37. Kf1 g5 38. Ke1 Kd4 39. Kd1 Rc7
40. Kd2 Rd7 41. Ke2 g4 42. Kd1 Re7 43. Kc2 Rd7 44. Kd1 Kd3 45. Ke1
Rb7 46. Kf1 Rb1#

Notes

Game 6

1. Nf3 d5 2. e4 dxe4 3. Bc4 b6 4. 0-0 c6 5. Nc3 Nf6 6. d4 e6 7. Bf4 Ke7
8. a4 Bb7 9. b4 a6 10. Nxe4 Ng4 11. Nd6 Ra7 12. Ng5 b5 13. Qxg4 g6
14. Bxb5 cxb5 15. Ngxf7 Qb6 16. Qg5+ Kd7 17. axb5 Be7 18. Qxe7+
Kxe7 19. d5 axb5 20. Bg5+ Kf8 21. dxe6 Qd4 22. e7+ Kg7 23. Bh6+ Kf6
24. c3 Qd5 25. c4 Qxg2#

Notes

Game 7

1. e4 e5 2. Bc4 Nf6 3. Nf3 Bd6 4. 0-0 Qe7 5. d3 Qf8 6. Bg5 Rg8 7. Nc3 Nc6 8. a4 h6 9. b4 a6 10. b5 Na5 11. b6 hxg5 12. bxc7 Nxc4 13. Nxg5 Nb2 14. Qb1 Bc5 15. Qxb2 Rh8 16. Nd5 Bd6 17. Rae1 Rh6 18. a5 Qg8 19. c4 Ra7 20. c5 Nxd5 21. Nf3 Rg6 22. Nh4 Bxc7 23. d4 Rg4 24. c6 dxc6 25. exd5 Bd7 26. d6 Bd8 27. d5 Rxh4 28. Rxe5+ Kf8 29. Re7 Bxe7 30. dxc6 Bxc6 31. Qb6 Ra8 32. Qc5 Bd8 33. d7+ Be7 34. Qe3 Rg4 35. Qxe7+ Kxe7 36. d8=Q+ Rxd8 37. Re1+ Kf8 38. Rf1 Rxg2+ 39. Kh1 Rxf2+ 40. Kg1 Rg2+ 41. Kh1 Rg3+ 42. Rf3 Bxf3#

Notes

Game 8

1. e4 e5 2. Bc4 Nf6 3. Nf3 Nc6 4. 0-0 g6 5. d3 Nh5 6. Bg5 Nf6 7. Bxf6 Qxf6 8. d4 exd4 9. Nc3 g5 10. Nd5 Qg6 11. Nxd4 Bd6 12. Nf5 a6 13. Nxd6+ Qxd6 14. a4 0-0 15. b4 Nd8 16. b5 Rb8 17. bxa6 bxa6 18. Bxa6 Ne6 19. c3 Nf4 20. Rb1 Ra8 21. e5 Qxa6 22. Nxf4 gxf4 23. e6 Qxe6 24. c4 Qf5 25. c5 Ba6 26. a5 Rfd8 27. c6 Bxf1 28. Kxf1 dxc6 29. a6 Rxd1+ 30. Rxd1 Qb5+ 31. Kg1 Rxa6 32. Rd8+ Kg7 33. Rd1 Qa5 34. Rc1 Qa3 35. Rf1 Qc5 36. Re1 f5 37. Rf1 Qd6 38. Kh1 Rb6 39. Kg1 Rb8 40. Re1 c5 41. Kh1 Kg6 42. Kg1 Kg7 43. Rd1 Qxd1#

Notes

Game 9

1. e4 c5 2. Bc4 g5 3. Nf3 g4 4. 0-0 Bh6 5. Nc3 Na6 6. d3 Bg7 7. Bf4 d6 8. Nd5 Be6 9. a4 Bd7 10. b4 gxf3 11. c3 cxb4 12. a5 fxg2 13. Bxa6 gxf1=Q+ 14. Qxf1 Bc8 15. Bxb7 Bxb7 16. c4 Bxa1 17. Bxd6 Bxd5 18. exd5 Qxa5 19. Bxe7 Kxe7 20. d6+ Kxd6 21. c5+ Kc7 22. c6 Rc8 23. d4 b3 24. d5 Rd8 25. d6+ Kb6 26. c7 Re8 27. c8=Q Rxc8 28. d7 Ra8 29. d8=Q+ Rxd8 30. Qd1 Rxd1+ 31. Kg2 h5 32. h4 Qa4 33. f3 Qxh4 34. f4 Rc1 35. Kf3 a6 36. Ke3 Ne7 37. Ke2 b2 38. f5 Re1+ 39. Kf3 Qg4+ 40. Kf2 Re2+ 41. Kf1 b1=Q#

Notes

Game 10

1. e4 e5 2. Bc4 Nf6 3. Nf3 d6 4. 0-0 Nxe4 5. d3 Nc5 6. Bf4 Na4 7. Nc3 Nxc3 8. bxc3 exf4 9. a4 Qe7 10. d4 Bf5 11. Qe1 a6 12. Ng5 c6 13. Bxf7+ Kd7 14. Nxh7 Qxf7 15. Rb1 Kc7 16. Qd2 Bxh7 17. c4 Kc8 18. d5 Nd7 19. dxc6 bxc6 20. c5 Nxc5 21. c4 Bxb1 22. Rxb1 Ra7 23. Rf1 Qxc4 24. a5 Rb7 25. Qd1 Qa4 26. Qg4+ Kb8 27. Qc8+ Kxc8 28. Rc1 Re7 29. Rf1 Rg8 30. Ra1 Qxa1#

Notes

Game 11

1. e4 e5 2. Bc4 Nf6 3. Nf3 d5 4. 0-0 dxc4 5. Nxe5 Qd6 6. d4 Be6 7. Bf4
c6 8. Nc3 a5 9. a4 Na6 10. b4 axb4 11. Nd5 Nxe4 12. Bg5 Nxg5 13. c3
cxd5 14. cxb4 g6 15. Nxf7 bxf7 16. Rc1 Qxb4 17. Rxc4 dxc4 18. d5 h6
19. a5 0-0-0 20. d6 h5 21. d7+ Kc7 22. Qd6+ Bxd6 23. Re1 Qxe1#

Notes

Game 12

1. e4 e5 2. Bc4 Nf6 3. Nf3 Bd6 4. 0-0 Ke7 5. Nc3 c6 6. d3 a6 7. Be3 Qg8
8. Ng5 Qd8 9. Bxa6 Rxa6 10. Nd5+ cxd5 11. d4 dxe4 12. dxe5 Bxe5 13.
Bc5+ d6 14. Bxd6+ Rxd6 15. Qxd6+ Bxd6 16. Nxe4 Qe8 17. Nxf6 Kxf6
18. Rae1 Be6 19. Rd1 Qc6 20. a4 Kg6 21. b4 b6 22. c4 Rf8 23. b5 Qd7
24. a5 bxa5 25. c5 Bxh2+ 26. Kxh2 Qxb5 27. c6 Qxc6 28. Rc1 Bc4 29.
Rcd1 a4 30. Ra1 Bxf1 31. Rxa4 Qxg2#

Notes

Game 13

1. e4 c5 2. Bc4 h5 3. Nf3 g6 4. 0-0 Nf6 5. d4 Nxe4 6. Bf4 f5 7. Nc3 e6 8.
Qe2 cxd4 9. Rad1 dxc3 10. b3 Qb6 11. a3 Ke7 12. a4 Rg8 13. b4 d6 14.
Ng5 d5 15. a5 Qxb4 16. Bxd5 Nc5 17. a6 Nbxa6 18. Bxe6 Bxe6 19. Bd6+
Ke8 20. Bxf8 Qb6 21. Rd6 Kxf8 22. Rd8+ Rxd8 23. Qf3 Na4 24. Nh7+
Ke7 25. Ng5 N6c5 26. Qf4 Qa6 27. Qe3 h4 28. Nf3 g5 29. Nxg5 b6 30.
Qf4 Qc4 31. Qe3 Rc8 32. Qxc5+ Nxc5 33. Nf3 Kf6 34. Ng5 Rxg5 35.
Re1 Qg4 36. Kf1 Bc4+ 37. Kg1 Qxg2#

Notes

Game 14

1. e4 c5 2. Bc4 h5 3. Nf3 g6 4. 0-0 d6 5. Nc3 a6 6. d4 Nh6 7. Bf4 f6 8.
a4 g5 9. b4 Ng4 10. Rc1 cxd4 11. Nxg5 fxg5 12. Bxg5 Bg7 13. Nd5 Nc6
14. b5 Nge5 15. bxa6 Nxc4 16. Nf6+ exf6 17. Qe1 Ra7 18. Rd1 fxg5 19. c3
bxa6 20. cxd4 0-0 21. e5 Re7 22. exd6 Rxe1 23. Rdxe1 Nxd6 24. d5 Ne5
25. a5 Qd7 26. Rxe5 Bxe5 27. Re1 Bb2 28. Rb1 Bg7 29. Rb8 Be5 30. Rb1
Nc4 31. Rc1 Nxa5 32. Ra1 Bxa1 33. d6 Kg7 34. Kf1 Bc3 35. Kg1 Ba1 36.
Kf1 Bc3 37. Kg1 h4 38. Kh1 g4 39. Kg1 Kf6 40. Kf1 Qb5+ 41. Kg1 Qb1#

Notes

Game 15

1. e4 c5 2. Bc4 d6 3. Nf3 b6 4. 0-0 Bd7 5. Nc3 e6 6. d3 Qc7 7. Bf4 Nc6
8. Rc1 Nb8 9. a4 a5 10. b3 h5 11. Ng5 Qb7 12. Qxh5 Rxh5 13. Nf3 Qc8
14. Bxe6 fxe6 15. Nd5 Qd8 16. Nc7+ Qxc7 17. Bxd6 Bxd6 18. c4 Bxh2+
19. Kh1 Bf4+ 20. Kg1 Bxc1 21. Rxc1 Qc8 22. Ne5 Rh7 23. Rf1 Qd8 24.
Nxd7 Qc7 25. d4 Qh2#

Notes

Game 16

1. e4 d5 2. Bc4 dxc4 3. Nf3 Bg4 4. 0-0 Bc6 5. Nc3 Nf6 6. d4 h6 7. Bf4
Qb8 8. a4 Qc8 9. b4 g5 10. Nd5 Bg7 11. Ne5 Bxd1 12. Nxc6 Nxd5 13.
Bg3 Nc3 14. e5 Bg4 15. d5 Bf5 16. a5 Nxd5 17. b5 Kf8 18. c3 bxc6 19.
e6 Bxe6 20. Bxc7 Qxc7 21. b6 axb6 22. axb6 Nxb6 23. Rad1 g4 24. Rc1
Rg8 25. Ra1 Rxa1 26. Rxa1 Bf6 27. Rf1 Bd5 28. Rd1 Bxc3 29. Rc1 Bb2
30. Rc2 Be5 31. Re2 c5 32. Rc2 Be4 33. Re2 Bd5 34. Rxe5 Qxe5 35. Kf1
Rg6 36. Kg1 Qa1#

Notes

Game 17

1. e4 e5 2. Bc4 Nc6 3. Nf3 Bc5 4. 0-0 Nf6 5. Nxe5 Nxe5 6. Qh5 Nxh5 7. d4 Bxd4 8. Bf4 Nxf4 9. Nc3 Nxc4 10. b3 Nd2 11. Nd5 Nxd5 12. a4 Nf6 13. b4 Nh5 14. c3 Bxc3 15. Ra3 Bxb4 16. Rh3 g6 17. Rxh5 gxh5 18. e5 Nxf1 19. Kxf1 0-0 20. a5 Qh4 21. e6 Qc4+ 22. Kg1 Qc1#

Notes

Game 18

1. Nf3 Nf6 2. e4 Rg8 3. Bc4 c6 4. 0-0 Nxe4 5. d4 d6 6. b4 g6 7. a4 Nd7
8. Bf4 Ndf6 9. Nc3 Nxc3 10. Ra3 Nxd1 11. Rd3 Nb2 12. Bxf7+ Kxf7
13. a5 Nxd3 14. Ng5+ Kg7 15. Bxd6 exd6 16. b5 cxb5 17. c4 bxc4 18. d5
Qe8 19. Nxh7 Ng4 20. a6 Kxh7 21. axb7 Bxb7 22. Rd1 g5 23. Rxd3 Qe1#

Notes

Game 19

1. Nf3 Nf6 2. e4 Nh5 3. Bc4 c5 4. 0-0 Nc6 5. d4 f5 6. Bh6 gxh6 7. Nc3 Nf4 8. Ne5 cxd4 9. Nd5 Nxe5 10. exf5 d3 11. Nxe7 Ne2+ 12. Kh1 Qxe7 13. f6 Qxf6 14. a4 Qh4 15. b4 Nc3 16. a5 Nxd1 17. b5 dxc2 18. a6 Qxc4 19. axb7 Qxf1#

Notes

Game 20

1. Nf3 d5 2. e4 d4 3. Bc4 Qd6 4. 0-0 Na6 5. e5 Qc5 6. e6 fxe6 7. Ne5
Qxe5 8. Bxe6 Bxe6 9. d3 0-0-0 10. Bg5 Qxg5 11. Nd2 b5 12. Ne4 Qh4
13. a4 Qg4 14. axb5 Nf6 15. c4 Qxd1 16. b4 Qxd3 17. Rad1 Qxe4 18.
bxa6 Qg4 19. c5 Qe2 20. b5 Ng4 21. b6 c6 22. Rde1 Qa2 23. bxa7 Kc7
24. Ra1 Qd5 25. Rad1 Qxc5 26. Rxd4 Qxd4 27. a8=Q Rxa8 28. a7 Qxa7
29. Rad1 Qxa1#

Notes

Game 21

1. e4 c5 2. Bc4 b6 3. Nf3 Na6 4. 0-0 Nb8 5. d4 Nf6 6. Ne5 e6 7. Bg5 h6
8. Nc3 cxd4 9. Bxf6 gxf6 10. Qxd4 fxe5 11. Qxe5 Rg8 12. Bxe6 dxe6 13.
Nd5 Qd6 14. Nc7+ Kd8 15. a4 Qxe5 16. b4 Qxc7 17. c4 Bd7 18. c5 h5
19. cxb6 axb6 20. a5 Qa7 21. axb6 Qxa1 22. b7 Ra4 23. e5 Qc3 24. b5
Qf3 25. b6 Qxg2#

Notes

Game 22

1. e4 e5 2. Bc4 Nc6 3. Nf3 Bc5 4. 0-0 Bf6 5. Nc3 d6 6. d4 Bxd4 7. Bg5 Bc5 8. a4 a6 9. b4 Bb6 10. Nd5 Bd4 11. Nxe5 dxe5 12. c3 Qd6 13. Qh5 Nxh5 14. Nxc7+ Qxc7 15. b5 axb5 16. a5 Rb8 17. Bxb5 Bc5 18. a6 b6 19. a7 Ra8 20. Bxc6+ Qxc6 21. Rab1 Rxa7 22. Ra1 Ba6 23. Rxa6 Rxa6 24. Bf4 Nxf4 25. c4 Ra8 26. Ra1 Rxa1#

Notes

Game 23

1. e4 e5 2. Bc4 Nf6 3. Nf3 Nxe4 4. 0-0 Rg8 5. Nc3 Nxc3 6. d4 Nxd1 7. dxe5 Bb4 8. Bg5 Nxb2 9. Bxf7+ Kxf7 10. Nd4 Qxg5 11. c3 Ba5 12. c4 Nxc4 13. a3 Qxe5 14. Rae1 Qxd4 15. Rd1 Qc3 16. Rc1 Qd4 17. Rcd1 Qc3 18. Rd3 Qxd3 19. a4 d6 20. Rd1 Qxd1#

Notes

Game 24

1. e4 e6 2. Bc4 Na6 3. Nf3 c6 4. 0-0 Qc7 5. d4 Nh6 6. Bg5 Nb4 7. Nc3 Rb8 8. Bxh6 Qb6 9. a3 gxh6 10. Ne5 Na6 11. Bxa6 Be7 12. Bb5 bxa6 13. Nc7+ Qxc7 14. a4 Rxb2 15. c4 a5 16. Nxc6 Qxc6 17. d5 Qc7 18. dxe6 dxe6 19. Rb1 Rxb1 20. c5 Rxd1 21. c6 Rxf1+ 22. Kxf1 Bf8 23. e5 Qxe5 24. c7 Ba6+ 25. Kg1 Qa1#

Notes

Game 25

1. Nf3 Nf6 2. e4 d6 3. Bc4 Nxe4 4. 0-0 c6 5. Nc3 Nc5 6. d4 Nca6 7. Bf4 b6 8. d5 c5 9. Ne5 Bb7 10. Bxa6 Qc7 11. a4 Nxa6 12. b4 cxb4 13. Nxf7 h6 14. Bxd6 Qc8 15. a5 exd6 16. axb6 Kxf7 17. Nb5 axb6 18. Nxd6+ Bxd6 19. c3 h5 20. cxd4 Qe8 21. Rxa6 Bxa6 22. b5 Bc8 23. Qf3+ Kg8 24. Qc3 Qd7 25. Qd3 Qd8 26. Qc2 Qg5 27. Qe4 Bf5 28. Qe8+ Rxe8 29. Kh1 Be4 30. Rg1 Qxd5 31. Rd1 Qxd1#

Notes

5

Draw: Five Games

Game 1

1. e4 e5 2. Bc4 Nf6 3. Nf3 Nc6 4. 0-0 Bd6 5. Nc3 h6 6. d4 exd4 7. Nb5
Nxe4 8. Qe2 Qe7 9. Nfxd4 Nxd4 10. Nxd4 a5 11. Nf5 Qe5 12. Nxd6+
Qxd6 13. Qxe4+ Qe7 14. Qd4 f5 15. Bf4 d6 16. Rae1 Be6 17. Rxe6 Rh7
18. Rxe7+ Kxe7 19. Bxd6+ cxd6 20. Qd5 Rc8 21. Qe6+ Kd8 22. Qxd6+
Ke8 23. Qe6+ Kd8 24. Qb6+ Ke7 25. Qe6+ Kd8 26. Qf7 Rc6 27. Qxb7
Rxc4 28. Qd5+ Kc7 29. Qxa5+ Kc6 30. a4 Rc5 31. b4 Rxa5 32. bxa5 Kc7
33. a6 Rh8 34. a5 Re8 35. c4 Rf8 36. c5 h5 37. a7 h4 38. a6 Rg8 39. Ra1
g5 40. a8=Q Rxa8 41. a7 Kc6 42. Rc1 g4 43. Ra1 f4 44. Ra5 Kb7 45.
Ra4 f3 46. Ra1 h3 47. c6+ Kxc6 48. Ra6+ Kb7 49. Ra3 hxg2 50. h4 Rf8
51. a8=Q+ Rxa8 52. Rxa8 Kxa8 53. Kh2 Ka7 54. h5 Ka8 55. Kg1 Kb8
56. h6 Ka7 57. h7 Kb8 58. h8=Q+ Kb7 59. Qg7+ Kc6 60. Qxg4 Kb6 61.
Qxf3 Ka7 62. Kxg2 Kb8 63. Qc6 Ka7 64. f4 Kb8 65. f5 Ka7 66. f6 Kb8
67. f7 Ka7 68. f8=Q

Notes

Game 2

1. e4 e5 2. Bc4 Nf6 3. Nf3 Qe7 4. 0-0 Qd6 5. Ng5 c6 6. Nxf7 Qb4 7. Bb3 Nxe4 8. Nxh8 g6 9. Nf7 Qa5 10. d4 exd4 11. Qxd4 Qf5 12. Nd2 Qf6 13. Qe3 d5 14. Nxe4 Qe6 15. Ned6+ Bxd6 16. Nxd6+ Kd8 17. Qh6 Qxd6 18. Bf4 Qf6 19. Bg5 Qxg5 20. Qxg5+ Kd7 21. Rae1 Kc7 22. Re8 Nd7 23. Qd8+ Kd6 24. Qe7+ Kc7 25. Qd8+ Kd6 26. Qe7+ Kc7 27. Qd8+

Notes

Game 3

1. Nf3 Nf6 2. e4 d6 3. Bc4 Qd7 4. 0-0 b5 5. Nc3 bxc4 6. d4 Ng8 7. Qe2
Nf6 8. e5 d5 9. exf6 gxf6 10. Bf4 Bb7 11. b3 a6 12. Rae1 Bc6 13. bxc4
Bb7 11. b3 a6 12. Rae1 Bc6 13. bxc4 Bb7 14. Nxd5 Bxd5 15. cxd5 Kd8
16. c4 f5 17. Rb1 f6 18. Rb7 Qc8 19. Rxc7 Qxc7 20. Bxc7+ Kxc7 21. Qe6
h6 22. c5 Rh7 23. Qb6+ Kc8 24. Qe6+ Kd8 25. Qb6+ Kc8 26. Qe6+
Kd8 27. Qb6+ Kc8

Notes

Game 4

1. e4 c5 2. Bc4 Na6 3. Nf3 g6 4. 0-0 Nb4 5. d4 d5 6. exd5 b6 7. dxc5
Qc7 8. c3 Qxc5 9. Na3 Na6 10. Bxa6 Bxa6 11. Qa4+ Kd8 12. Ne5 Qxd5
13. Nxf7+ Qxf7 14. Qxa6 Qd5 15. Qa4 a6 16. Be3 Qd6 17. Bxb6+ Qxb6
18. Nc4 Qb5 19. Qxb5 axb5 20. Ne5 Kc7 21. Nf7 e6 22. Nxh8 Bc5 23.
Nf7 Kb6 24. b4 Be7 25. Rae1 Kc7 26. Rxe6 Rb8 27. Ne5 Bh4 28. c4 h6
29. cxb5 Rxb5 30. a4 Rd5 31. b5 Bg5 32. a5 Bd8 33. b6+ Kb7 34. Nc6
Bf6 35. a6+ Kxa6 36. Nb4+ Kb7 37. Nxd5 Bh4 38. Rxg6 Bg5 39. Rxg8
h5 40. Rg7+ Kc6 41. Rxg5 Kd7 42. b7 Kc6 43. b8=Q h4 44. Nb6 h3 45.
Rg6+ Kb5 46. Rg5+ Kb4 47. Qg3 hxg2 48. Kxg2

Notes

Game 5

1. Nf3 e6 2. e4 Nf6 3. Bc4 c5 4. 0-0 b6 5. d4 Qc7 6. Ng5 a6 7. Bxf7+ Kd8 8. dxc5 b5 9. e5 Qxc5 10. exf6 gxf6 11. Be3 Qf5 12. Bb6+ Kd7 13. Be6+ Qxe6 14. Nxe6 b4 15. Qf3 Nc6 16. Nc5+ dxc5 17. Nd2 e6 18. Rae1 f5 19. b3 Rb8 20. Bxc5 Bxc5 21. Nc4 Nd4 22. Rd1 h6 23. Qg3 Bb7 24. Qg7+ Kc6 25. Rxd4 Bc8 26. Qxh8 Kb7 27. Rd8 Ra8 28. Qg7+ Kc6 29. Qxh6 Re7 30. Rxc8+ Rxc8 31. Qxe6+ Kc7 32. Qxe7+ Kb8 33. Qe6 Rc7 34. Qxa6 Rg7 35. Qf6 Rc7 36. Qxf5 Rc6 37. Qe5+ Kc8 38. Na5 Rc3 39. Qe2 Kb8 40. a3 Rxc2 41. Qxc2 bxa3 42. Qc1 a2 43. Qa1 Ka8 44. Qxa2 Ka7 45. b4 Kb6 46. Qc4 Ka7 47. b5 Kb8 48. Qc5 Ka8 49. b6 Kb8 50. Qc6

Notes

CONCLUSION

The fundamental problem with relying too much on information technology (IT) or artificial intelligence (AI) is that technology is a two-dimensional world, and we live in a three-dimensional world. The three-dimensional world has human emotions such as the will to live, survive, and thrive, which could be some of the strongest forces in the universe.

At the highest level, IT and AI cannot calculate or forecast the will to live, sacrifice, or be sacrificed. They also cannot calculate or forecast the will to work hard, never quit, and win. According to the science of noetics in Dan Brown's *The Lost Symbol*, the mind can physically and materially change matter because the mind can change the world around us from the subatomic level to the molecular level and beyond. When a human plays a fellow human, IT and AI should be placed in deference to hard work, never quitting, and the will to win.

An analysis of the five hundred games I played presents the following conclusions: In 420 games, the bunker was not busted, and the game was won. In fifty games, the bunker was busted, and the game was won. In twenty-five games, the bunker was busted, and the game was lost. In five games, the game was a draw. In universal summary, the King's Bunker Strategy provides beginners with a highly effective defense strategy, thereby giving beginners confidence to play chess as a means of happiness for a lifetime.

Concluding Mantra: Play chess. Be happy.
Never quit. Be of virtue.

AFTERWORD

The Queen's Victory Opening: An Attack Strategy for Beginners—furthers my contributions to chess, the greatest game in the world, past, present, and future—and instills happiness in those who play chess for a lifetime.

Order of Battle

Enemy: The opponent's king is priceless and is the key to victory.

Intelligence: As with any intelligence-gathering effort, it is imperative to discover what strategies, tactics, and specific moves your opponent is currently—today, at this very moment—practicing.

Friendly: A hyperaggressive opening using your queen on the second move to attack and continuously pursue the opponent's king to victory.

Mission: Checkmate the opponent's king and bring him to justice.

Execution: King's Pawn Opening, e4, followed by your queen attacking the opponent's king side, Qh5. Keep your queen focused on attacking the opponent's king and checkmate with your queen.

Command and Control: Unique Contribution: The strategy of beginning the attack with your queen and winning the battle with her by checkmating the opponent's king with your queen.

QueensVictoryOpening.com website is an accounting of my chess wins using the hyperaggressive Queen's Victory Opening in order to instill confidence, sustain hard work, and never quit for a lifetime of happiness. It's all about happiness!

REFERENCES

Books

How Life Imitates Chess: Garry Kasparov
Chess Fundamentals: Jose Raul Capablanca
The Modern Chess Instructor: Wilhelm Steinitz
My System & Chess Praxis: Aron Nimzowitsch
Three Hundred Chess Games: Siegbert Tarrasch
The Modernized Grunfeld Defense: Yaroslav Zherebukh
The Lost Symbol: Dan Brown

Clubs

Chess Club and Scholastic Center of Atlanta

Websites and Associations

Chess.com: *Queen's Gambit* predecessor
LiChess.com: Bernard Arnault and Thibault Duplessis
Chess24.com: Magnus Carlsen
Wikipedia.com: Research
Google.com: Research
arXiv.org: Research
QueensVictoryOpening.com: Follow-up contribution
Unibet.com: Magnus Carlsen
Skilling.com: Magnus Carlsen

Online Education

MasterClass Series

ABOUT THE AUTHOR

Robert W. Bradshaw took his first chess lesson from Garry Kasparov who inspired him to play chess as a lifelong journey of happiness. Likewise, in order to inspire other beginners to play chess for a lifetime, Robert played five hundred games to validate his hypermodern thesis that the best offense is a better defense. Robert presents inspiring analysis and conclusions to sustain chess beginners in their lifetime journey of happiness.

Play chess. Be happy.
Never quit. Be of virtue.

Printed in the United States
by Baker & Taylor Publisher Services